MW01243126

His Blood Is Our Confession

The Blood of Jesus

Sam Hager

Title ID: 5506542

ISBN-10: 1512262250
ISBN-13: 978-1512262254

Cover design - Karla Bradley

HIS BLOOD IS OUR CONFESSION

CONTENTS

Foreword

The love of God for humanity is passionate, intense and unrelenting. He conceived us before time began and has planned a destiny of freedom, glory, and power in union with Him for each one.

There is, however, a diabolical spirit at work behind the scenes; a created spirit who has willfully turned his back on God and has dedicated himself to robbing humanity of her destiny. Satan, the devil, the accuser, the "light-bearer" as he is called, is a deceiver, a dream stealer, a killer and destroyer. He is the god behind the world's system, which is why with every decade of celebrated "advancement," there is a growing emptiness, confusion and decay in the world.

As human beings, created with a great destiny to be co-heirs with Christ, the Father allows every searching heart to go through a process of true discovery. An unfolding realization about who we are and what is available to us to overcome every destructive process our enemy, Satan, aims to bring into our lives. This discovery enables us to take our place at His right hand with His Son, Jesus Christ.

Sounds incredible, doesn't it? That is because our world-system "education" dulls our minds to our true spiritual heritage and renders us ineffective against a diabolical unseen enemy. We need true education.

That is why I am so excited about this book. In modern language, it strips away the veil and introduces the reader to a world of reality; to a truth which was the bedrock of early Christian thought, and formed the foundation of faith and victory in the lives of those that have gone before us.

The admonition of the Lord to us today remains the same as it was in the days of Jeremiah when He said, "This is what the Lord says: 'Stop at the crossroads and look around. Ask for the old, godly way, and walk in it. Travel its path, and you will find rest for your souls... '" Jeremiah 6:16 (NLT)

We have the opportunity to travel a path of rest and victory; an ancient path, in these modern times.

The victory of every Christian today hinges on living in the truth that the Lord revealed through His angel who shouted with a loud voice across the heavens in the Revelation of John: "...For the accuser of our brothers and sisters has been thrown down to the earth... And they have defeated him by the blood of the Lamb and by their testimony. And they did not love their lives so much that they were afraid to die." Revelation 12:10-11 (NLT)

This is God's recipe for our victory. Let us learn together and embrace the truth concerning the blood of Christ, the Lamb of God. Let us daily appropriate its potency for our victorious living as we walk into the inheritance pre-destined for us by our loving Father.

I recommend this book to you. Study it. Meditate on it. Live victorious.

-Carlton Williams, Pastor of High Life Lagos

Preface

The day of Easter 2015, while at a church service celebrating the death, burial, and resurrection of Christ, God placed something in my heart. He wanted me to begin teaching on the blood of Jesus. At the time, I operated as the youth pastor for a church in Lagos, Nigeria. That same week I began researching the scriptures concerning the blood of Jesus. I was not previously unaware of the power of His blood, but God started pouring fresh revelation and understanding into my heart. Things became more real and clear to me as I intently studied the precious blood of Christ.

The following two Sundays after Easter of that year, I taught on this subject to the teenagers at High Life Church. The message was well received by students and adult leaders alike. After the series' conclusion, God continued expanding my understanding and recognition of the importance of the blood of Jesus. With all of the revelation I had been given, I felt inspired to write this book.

Whether or not you are a Christian, it is my sincere belief that furthering your knowledge of the blood of Jesus has the power to transform your life! My hope is that you will be comforted, encouraged, and refreshed as we take an in-depth look at this matter together.

May God richly bless you!

-Sam Hager

Chapter One
His Blood Speaks

The blood of Jesus speaks good things to God on our behalf, washes our sins away, gives us life, and seals a new covenant with God and humanity.

Before we look at verses dealing with the blood of Jesus directly, we need to get some helpful background information. First, let's investigate what blood is composed of. WebMD.com shares this about blood:

"Blood is a constantly circulating fluid providing the body with nutrition, oxygen, and waste removal. Blood is mostly liquid, with numerous cells and proteins suspended in it, making blood "thicker" than pure water. The average person has about 5 liters (more than a gallon) of blood.

A liquid called plasma makes up about half of the content of blood. Plasma contains

proteins that help blood to clot, transport substances through the blood, and perform other functions. Blood plasma also contains glucose and other dissolved nutrients. About half of blood volume is composed of blood cells:

• Red blood cells, which carry oxygen to the tissues
• White blood cells, which fight infections
• Platelets, smaller cells that help blood to clot

Blood is conducted through blood vessels (arteries and veins). Blood is prevented from clotting in the blood vessels by their smoothness, and the finely tuned balance of clotting factors."

Now let's look at the first recorded event in which someone killed another person, the story of Adam and Eve's first two sons; Cain and Abel.

Genesis 4:3-10
And in the process of time it came to pass that Cain brought an offering of the fruit of the ground to the Lord. 4 Abel also brought of the firstborn of his flock and of their fat. And the Lord respected Abel and his offering, 5 but He did not respect Cain and his offering. And Cain was very angry, and his countenance fell.

6 So the Lord said to Cain, "Why are you angry? And why has your countenance fallen? 7 If you do well, will you not be accepted? And if you do not do well, sin lies at the door. And its desire is for you, but you should rule over it."

8 Now Cain talked with Abel his brother; and it came to pass, when they were in the field, that Cain rose up against Abel his brother and killed him.

9 Then the Lord said to Cain, "Where is Abel your brother?"

He said, "I do not know. Am I my brother's keeper?"

10 And He said, "What have you done? The voice of your brother's blood cries out to Me from the ground. 11 So now you are cursed from the earth, which has opened its mouth to receive your brother's blood from your hand."

Notice that the ground opened its mouth to receive Abel's blood. Abel was murdered unfairly and without just cause. The Bible says that Abel's blood cried out to God. God Himself said that Abel's blood had a voice!

It seems strange to consider blood as being vocal. How can blood speak? What does it say? We know that medically speaking, blood reveals a lot of things to nurses and doctors. Through extracting blood from a patient, tests can be conducted to tell the medical staff many things about the health of the individual. In addition to medical science, blood speaks volumes to criminal investigators. Just as hospitals can evaluate certain things about the blood of patients, investigators have laboratories and forensic scientists to help solve criminal cases.

We may not be able to hear the voice of blood with our ears, but God allows us to determine a lot through analyzing it. With God nothing is impossible! He can hear the voice of blood. He has given us some insight in His Word.

Hebrews 12:24
to Jesus the Mediator of the new covenant, and to the blood of sprinkling that speaks better things than that of Abel.

The blood of Jesus speaks better things than the blood of Abel. So what did Abel's blood say? It probably spoke of injustice, and of the guilt of Cain. God declared that Cain was cursed after hearing the cry of Abel's blood.

Genesis 4:10-11
And He said, "What have you done? The voice of your brother's blood cries out to Me from the ground. 11 So now you are cursed from the earth, which has opened its mouth to receive your brother's blood from your hand."

The blood of Jesus speaks better things! What does the blood of Jesus say? For one, it speaks of forgiveness. Notice what Jesus said while giving His life on the cross.

Luke 23:34

Then Jesus said, "Father, forgive them, for they do not know what they do."

The plan of God was for Jesus to give His life as a sacrifice for the sins of humanity. Jesus agreed and willingly laid His life down, fulfilling His Father's plan. Jesus brought His blood to the altar in Heaven, which speaks for sinful, guilty humanity, **"Father, forgive them, for they do not know what they do."**

This is the one and only sacrifice that the Father God recognizes. Understand that Jesus is the only way to the Father. The blood of Jesus speaks forgiveness. This is not forced on people. We can freely receive forgiveness by calling on Jesus to save us.

Cain was guilty of Abel's death. The blood of Abel testified to this. If we are honest we would conclude that we are all guilty of sins and mistakes.

Romans 3:23
for all have sinned and fall short of the glory of God,

Maybe we have not killed anyone, but we wished certain people would die. That's sinful. The things we have stolen from others make us guilty of theft. The lies we've told have misled people. Ultimately, these sins make us guilty.

Romans 6:23
For the wages of sin is death, but the gift of God is eternal life in Christ Jesus our Lord.

Wages are what we earn. Since we have sinned we have earned death. We are guilty and therefore deserve to die. When Adam and Eve rebelled against God by eating what He had forbidden, they died spiritually. This spiritual death passed on through the generations of humanity. You and I inherited a fallen nature.

But God in His goodness offers us a gift. **Romans 6:32b "but the gift of God is eternal life in Christ Jesus our Lord."**

Gifts are something given for free. You do not work for gifts. If you work for it then you earn it. Earning wages and receiving gifts are different.

I can remember calling on Jesus to save me when I was about nine or ten years old. The Bible is clear: when you call on Jesus, He saves you. I experienced His forgiveness. I was baptized soon thereafter at Calvary Baptist Church in Walla Walla, Washington. There is nothing like experiencing the forgiveness of God! In His grace, He pardoned me. The blood of Jesus speaks better things than that of Abel's!

For some reason, at thirteen years old I lost my mind. During one summer, I visited a cousin in Oklahoma for a week or two. We walked together to one of his friend's houses, and I was introduced to smoking weed. I fell in love with getting high. I came to know it as herb, splif, green, toke, smoke, ganja, and of course marijuana. They also call it the gateway drug, which was an accurate description for me. My new-found friends had connections to obtain herb, but they also had connections to other things. It wasn't too long before I was introduced to crank, or methamphetamine. That became a different kind of thrill. Drugs that made me hallucinate captivated me. I deeply craved acid and shrooms. I rarely got my hands on these, but when I did, I willingly lost control to them.

Over my following teenage years, I successfully wrecked my life in serious ways. I stole from family and friends to buy drugs, which brought a lot of tension. My relationships became toxic through my own self-generated poison.

Years later when I was eighteen or nineteen, I found myself at Woodward Park in Tulsa, Oklahoma. I had just gotten stoned when four people all about my age started talking to me about God. They each had big smiles on their faces as they shared how Jesus had changed their lives. I told them that I believed in Jesus and knew He died on the cross for me. The four teenagers said they were glad that I knew Jesus and they were going to try to find some people who didn't. They left.

It's hard to describe what I felt when they walked away. It's like everything inside of me was hollow. My heart sank. It was a tremendous wake-up call! God was calling me to come home to Him! Although I had sabotaged my life, He still loved me and wanted me.

That weekend was a defining time for me. God changed my life by offering grace and forgiveness. His goodness brought me to change!

That was many years ago, and a lot has happened since that weekend. I can say without hesitation that I am extremely grateful to God and to those individuals who shared His love and hope with me. God knows who they are, even if I don't.

To those of you who shared your faith in Jesus with me, God bless you. It changed my life!

As I transition from my personal testimony back to this teaching on the blood of Jesus, let me say this; we are guilty. We deserve eternal death. God in His goodness offers us a gift that we do not deserve. This gift is eternal life. This gift comes through the forgiveness paid for with the blood of Jesus. If you recognize that Jesus poured out His blood to pay for your guilt, you can call on Him to save you and He will do it.

The blood of Jesus has a voice. His blood speaks of forgiveness. It speaks of eternal life. Does the blood of Jesus speak for you?

Chapter Two

His Blood Washes

The hymn "Nothing but the Blood" from Robert Lowry that was published in 1876 contains timeless truth, even though it was written in a language that is becoming antiquated. Here is the first verse:

> **"What can wash away my sin?**
> **Nothing but the blood of Jesus;**
> **What can make me whole again?**
> **Nothing but the blood of Jesus."**

It is eternally important to understand that there is nothing that can wash away your sin other than the blood of Jesus. God designed it this way. We have all sinned. Our sins have stained us. The guilt of what we have done has contaminated our inner selves. We need to be clean.

Sinful humanity cannot purify itself from sin. **Isaiah 64:6** says, **"But we are all like an** unclean thing, And all our righteousnesses are like filthy rags; We all fade as a leaf, And our iniquities, like the wind, Have taken us away."

There are a few things to acknowledge here.

1. **Our sin has made us unclean.**
2. **Our attempts to cleanse ourselves do not work.**

I've shared my faith in Jesus with a lot of people. It's amazing how many tell me that they'll go to Heaven because they are good people and they haven't killed anybody. If someone believes that they are going to Heaven because the good things they have done outnumber the bad things they have done, they are trusting in their filthy rags to wash their sins away. (Side note: You may be shocked to look up what that means in the original language. Filthy rags, literally translated, are menstrual cloths!) Generally, when someone says they will go to Heaven because they haven't killed anyone, I thank them. I say something like, "Thanks for not killing anyone. On behalf of humanity, I'm grateful for that." I then segue into talking about Jesus.

It comes down to this; you either trust yourself or you trust Jesus to make you clean before God. You either trust your righteousness as your way to approach God or you trust in the sacrifice of Jesus as your way to the Father.

I used to work in the printing industry, and befriended a co-worker who shared an interest in chess. We started playing games online against each other. Once the game had been set up, we would receive an email notification when our opponent had made their move, then we would have a set number of days to take our turn. These chess games could go on for weeks, even months. He always won the games, but in the process he taught me a lot and I'm a much stronger chess player as a result. This led us to talk more at work, and I learned something about him. He was trusting in his own righteousness to get him into Heaven.

He's a pretty good guy. I've never heard him cuss and I rarely even saw him get upset. He has always been polite and considerate. That's all well and good, but as I explained to him, he can't earn his way into Heaven.

I'll try to describe how God led me to communicate this truth to my friend. I played another online chess match with an opponent that I did not know personally. This guy had a pretty high rating, so I discussed the game with my co-worker. It lasted for over a month. My new opponent was tough! I couldn't make any mistakes and every move I made had to be calculated and analyzed carefully.

One particular night during praise and worship at a church in Broken Arrow, Oklahoma, I felt God speak to my spirit. He impressed on me to share my faith with my work friend the same day that I won the chess game with my competitor.

After church that night, I discovered that the guy I had been playing chess with resigned. This came as a complete surprise! I had the advantage in an end game scenario, but by no means did I have a clear path to a checkmate. He did not have to give up at that point, but he did. I won the game!

God had clearly told me to share my faith with my colleague the same day I won that game. So I wrote him an email through the chess site. I shared my testimony, woven together with verses about grace. I trusted God to guide my words as I let him know that he cannot trust himself to go to Heaven, but he must trust in Jesus alone. Jesus is the only way!

The next time we saw each other at work, he congratulated me on winning the chess game against the highly ranked player. He then told me that he was comfortable in his beliefs, and that he didn't want to talk about religion with me, but we could continue to talk about chess and work and other things.

This saddened me. I continued to be friendly with him, but our relationship did change after that. I pray that, at some point before it's too late, my friend realizes his desperate need for the loving God.

God loved the world so much that He sent His Son Jesus. Jesus is the way to God! We cannot wash away our sins; only the blood of Jesus can do that.

1 John 1:7
But if we walk in the light as He is in the light, we have fellowship with one another, and the blood of Jesus Christ His Son cleanses us from all sin.

God has revealed His plan to wash away our sins. This plan was fulfilled on the cross when His Son gave His life for you and me. The blood of Jesus poured out and paid for our eternal freedom!

Another part of that hymn by Robert Lowry goes like this:

> **"For my pardon, this I see,**
> **Nothing but the blood of Jesus;**
> **For my cleansing this my plea,**
> **Nothing but the blood of Jesus."**

Mr. Lowry apparently understood grace. Robert declared that he was not trusting in himself to become clean before God. He trusted only in the blood of Jesus. We need this revelation! Apart from Jesus we can do nothing! Our efforts and works do not make us right with God! When we come to God exalting ourselves, to Him we are rejecting His Son.

God loved the world so much that He gave His Son Jesus! Jesus gave His life so that you and I could be forgiven of all our sins and so we would not perish in our uncleanliness! If we arrogantly tell God that we don't need His Son, we will stay spiritually dead. If, however, we place our trust in Jesus we will become spiritually alive.

This is explained in **John 3:3** which says, **"Jesus answered and said to him, 'Most assuredly, I say to you, unless one is born again, he cannot see the kingdom of God.'"**

Jesus is telling us that we must be born again. This means that until we are born again we are not clean before God. We are spiritually dead without the blood of Jesus. We must be born again if we are to see the kingdom of God. The only way to become spiritually alive is through the blood of Jesus. We must trust God (not ourselves) to become clean. God gave His Son Jesus. Jesus gave

His life. If we call on Jesus we will be saved! The
sacrifice of Jesus has the power to make you clean.
God will not force anyone to believe. The blood of
Jesus speaks for you in Heaven. His blood is
available for you.

Hebrews 9:11-14

**But Christ came as High Priest of the good
things to come, with the greater and more
perfect tabernacle not made with hands, that
is, not of this creation. 12 Not with the blood
of goats and calves, but with His own blood He
entered the Most Holy Place once for all,
having obtained eternal redemption. 13 For if
the blood of bulls and goats and the ashes of a
heifer, sprinkling the unclean, sanctifies for
the purifying of the flesh, 14 how much more
shall the blood of Christ, who through the
eternal Spirit offered Himself without spot to
God, cleanse your conscience from dead works
to serve the living God?**

There is so much to elaborate on in the
aforementioned verses! For now, I want to focus
on the phrase **"cleanse your conscience from
dead works."** If you have placed your trust in
Jesus, embrace the truth of **Hebrews 9:14**. Your
very conscience can be washed totally clean
through the blood of Jesus! Even though you
committed dead works, the blood of Jesus speaks
forgiveness to God on your behalf. Through the

17

blood of Jesus, God sees you as pure! When you remember the past mistakes you have made, instead of a guilty conscience, you can have a thankful conscience. You can be grateful to God for the sacrifice of Jesus and let that dominate your thinking instead of the shame of sin. Instead of feeling guilty about your previous sins, let a holy sense of wonder flood your conscience. Rejoice in the goodness and forgiveness of God!

Isaiah 1:18
"Come now, and let us reason together,"
Says the Lord, "Though your sins are like scarlet, They shall be as white as snow; Though they are red like crimson, They shall be as wool."

God wants you to know that as you have received the blood of Jesus, you have the power to have a clean conscience. This spiritual freedom can envelop your soul! Let your mind be renewed with this truth. The blood of Jesus has washed your sins away! God sees you as spotless!

If God sees you as clean, you can see yourself this way too. To live at a higher level and walk in a clean conscience, it's important to renew and refresh your thoughts. The old thoughts and memories of the past mistakes you've made need to be counteracted by the living Word of God.

Romans 12:2

And do not be conformed to this world, but be transformed by the renewing of your mind, that you may prove what is that good and acceptable and perfect will of God.

Your body needs regular baths. Your mind does too! Your life can be transformed by renewing your mind with God's Word. Through this continual process of allowing the Word of God to wash your mind, you will be able to know the will of God.

Notice also that **Romans 12:2** talks about **"...that good and acceptable and perfect will of God."** There are things that God calls good. There are also things that are acceptable to Him. He acknowledges them and they are okay. Other things, He considers perfect. God gives us a lot of freedom to walk in! He doesn't want you to be uptight and walking on some difficult tight-rope. Be free and know that there are a lot of things that are good and acceptable and perfect to Him. He has good plans for you!

Continue to follow Jesus and get into the Word of God! This is how you will be able to distinguish and discern the way of life. With a renewed mind and clean conscience, you can see God at work on so many levels.

Matthew 5:8
Blessed are the pure in heart, For they shall see God.

The chorus for the great hymn by Robert Lowry goes like this:

"Oh! precious is the flow,
That makes me white as snow;
No other fount I know,
Nothing but the blood of Jesus."

Imagine! Though our sins have contaminated our lives, He offers forgiveness and spiritual cleanliness! Our consciousness can be cleansed and filled with gratitude. This has been made possible through the blood of Jesus.

Have you allowed the blood of Jesus to wash your sins away? Are you living your life with a conscience that is free from guilt?

Chapter Three
His Blood Gives Life

From RedCrossBlood.Org:

- Every two seconds someone in the U.S. needs blood.
- More than 41,000 blood donations are needed every day.
- A total of 30 million blood components are transfused each year in the U.S.
- The average red blood cell transfusion is approximately 3 pints.
- The blood type most often requested by hospitals is Type O.
- The blood used in an emergency is already on the shelves before the event occurs.
- Sickle cell disease affects more than 70,000 people in the U.S. About 1,000 babies are born with the disease each year. Sickle cell patients can require

frequent blood transfusions throughout their lives.

- More than 1.6 million people were diagnosed with cancer last year. Many of them will need blood, sometimes daily, during their chemotherapy treatment.
- A single car accident victim can require as many as 100 pints of blood.

As it is known, we need blood to live. When a person is drained of blood, they are also drained of life. Have you heard the slogan, "Save a life, give blood?" Jesus gave His blood, allowing His vitality to pour out for the salvation of many. He was giving His blood to save the world, and to give us life!

Jesus said some remarkable words at a synagogue in Capernaum.

John 6:53-58
Then Jesus said to them, "Most assuredly, I say to you, unless you eat the flesh of the Son of Man and drink His blood, you have no life in you. 54 Whoever eats My flesh and drinks My blood has eternal life, and I will raise him up at the last day. 55 For My flesh is food indeed, and My blood is drink indeed. 56 He who eats My flesh and drinks My blood abides in Me, and I in him. 57 As the living Father sent Me, and I live because of the Father, so he

who feeds on Me will live because of Me. 58 This is the bread which came down from heaven—not as your fathers ate the manna, and are dead. He who eats this bread will live forever."

Now this was a shocking thing to say! Many of His followers left Him because of this controversial statement. After they had gone, in verse 67 He asked His twelve disciples, **"Do you also want to go away?"** There were people who enjoyed hanging out with Jesus when they could see Him perform miracles, but they would not relinquish the throne of their hearts to His Lordship.

"Do you also want to go away?"

How do we respond to this? Our response to this has eternal consequences. There are a lot of people who refuse to believe that the blood of Jesus gives life. Many trust in their own sacrifices. Are we willing to follow Him and trust Him? Are we willing to get off of the throne in our hearts and let Jesus rule? There's a difference between knowing about Jesus and receiving Jesus.

John 6:53
Then Jesus said to them, "Most assuredly, I say to you, unless you eat the flesh of the Son of Man and drink His blood, you have no life in you.

The blood of Jesus gives life! If we don't have His blood, we don't have life! Once again, this goes back to the first man and woman, Adam and Eve, turning their backs to God and rejecting the truth. Sin entered them, corrupting their pure nature. This sinful nature passed through their offspring, and because of this, we are all born this way. We don't teach sinful behavior to toddlers. It comes to them naturally.

Genesis 2:16-17
And the Lord God commanded the man, saying, "Of every tree of the garden you may freely eat; 17 but of the tree of the knowledge of good and evil you shall not eat, for in the day that you eat of it you shall surely die."

Adam and Eve ate of this tree and in that very day they died. They continued to live physically for many years afterward, but understand that God tells the truth. They died spiritually that day.

To better understand this, let's look at **1 Thessalonians 5:23**, which says, **"Now may the God of peace Himself sanctify you completely; and may your whole spirit, soul, and body be preserved blameless at the coming of our Lord Jesus Christ."**

This verse reveals that we are completely

composed of three parts. We are triune beings, if you will. The Bible says, "**...and may your whole spirit, soul and body be preserved blameless...**" God sees you completely. Whether you or I fully understand this, He sees us in our entirety. He identifies your complete package as spirit, soul and body.

It's easy to understand that we have a body. You can see yours, but I suppose if you did not have the ability to see, you could feel your body. It's natural and it is easily identifiable.

Your soul is not your body and it is different from your spirit. This too should be easy to understand when you realize that your soul encompasses your mental faculties. This includes your willpower, intellect, and emotional capacities. In simplified terms, your soul is your mind, will, and emotions. Just as your body is unique, your soul, too, is one of a kind!

Your spirit is also a separate entity from the previous two. The Bible made a distinction between your spirit and soul. Another verse that highlights this is **Hebrews 4:12**, which says, "**For the word of God is living and powerful, and sharper than any two-edged sword, piercing even to the division of soul and spirit, and of joints and marrow, and is a discerner of the thoughts and intents of the heart.**" God's Word brings clarity in the fact that there is a difference between our souls and spirits.

Your spirit is your true self. At the core of your existence, you are a spirit. When Adam and Eve rebelled against God and ate from the forbidden tree, their spirits died. They perished spiritually. Though they continued to exist physically and mentally, they needed to be reborn spiritually. The way for this to happen would come through the blood of Jesus.

Skateboarding is fun for me. I really enjoy it! As I write this, I am in Lagos, Nigeria, where there are not that many places to skateboard. But that's okay. I knew that before I came, and I gladly accepted that reality because of the mission I embarked on with my family.

Once, several years ago, I was skateboarding along Riverside Drive in Tulsa, Oklahoma. I picked up momentum as I started rolling down a hill that went under a bridge. But my velocity increased even more! My board started shifting side to side and I lost control, flying off of my board and sliding down the pavement. As I hit the ground I remember shouting, "God...bless America!" When I finally stopped skidding on the asphalt, the skateboard came tumbling into me. Wham! It was a pretty bad crash. I remember thinking, "Did I just say God bless America?" I painfully got up and watched a drop of blood fall onto the skateboard. The griptape was blue, so the dark red was easy to see.

My point is this; blood is noticeable.

One thing that caught my attention from RedCrossBlood.Org was this; **"The blood used in an emergency is already on the shelves before the event occurs."** This is good planning. Before the immediate need, the solution is already on hand.

God is smart. He is a good planner. He provided the solution to our sin and death problem before we needed it.

I Peter 1:19-21
but with the precious blood of Christ, as of a lamb without blemish and without spot. 20 He indeed was foreordained before the foundation of the world, but was manifest in these last times for you 21 who through Him believe in God, who raised Him from the dead and gave Him glory, so that your faith and hope are in God.

God did not cause Adam and Eve to commit treason. They chose to rebel against God. They had a will to freely do as they wished. They chose to reject God's instructions and do what was forbidden. Though God did not force them to rebel, He already had the solution established in case of an emergency. The solution was (and is) the precious blood of Christ.

We need to be born again so we can become spiritually alive. This happens through the blood of Jesus being transfused into our spirits. This is how we become alive in God. We drink the blood of Jesus and live spiritually. Through receiving the blood of Jesus, we come alive!

The blood of Jesus abides on the altar of God. When we receive Jesus, we allow His blood to speak on our behalf, to cleanse us spiritually, and to give us life.

You have full access to God through the blood of Jesus. He wants you and I to draw near to Him. He desires a close relationship with you full of love and assurance. You can be assured that He loves you! He also wants your conscience to be cleansed from guilt! He wants you to live!

Psalm 34:8
Oh, taste and see that the Lord is good;
Blessed is the man who trusts in Him!

Chapter Four

His Blood Sealed

The blood of Jesus sealed the deal! What deal? He sealed the new deal, or you could say the new covenant.

To understand this, we should look at what a covenant means. From Dictionary.com, we find that a covenant is defined as; **"An agreement, usually formal, between two or more persons to do or not do something specified."**

Dictionary.com also states this about what a covenant means; **"A formal agreement of legal validity, especially one under seal."**

In simple terms, a covenant is a contract.

Jesus sealed the new covenant with His blood. For there to be a new covenant, there has to be an old one first, right?

Hebrews 8:7
For if that first covenant had been faultless,
then no place would have been sought for a
second.

Basically, there was a problem with the first
covenant. There was a fault.

Hebrews 8:8
Because finding fault with them, He says:
"Behold, the days are coming, says the Lord,
when I will make a new covenant with the
house of Israel and with the house of Judah—

Remember a covenant is an agreement. The
first covenant was an agreement with God and
humanity. The fault with the first covenant was
on humanity's side of the agreement. God kept up
His end, but people failed miserably!

Hebrews 8:9
not according to the covenant that I made
with their fathers in the day when I took them
by the hand to lead them out of the land of
Egypt; because they did not continue in My
covenant, and I disregarded them, says the
Lord.

The people did not do what was right. They
violated the contract in every way. This was the
fault of the first covenant. Fallen humanity cannot

do what they are supposed to do. Spiritually dead people cannot fulfill the requirements of a spiritually alive God.

Hebrews 8:10-13
For this is the covenant that I will make with the house of Israel after those days, says the Lord: I will put My laws in their mind and write them on their hearts; and I will be their God, and they shall be My people. 11 None of them shall teach his neighbor, and none his brother, saying, 'Know the Lord,' for all shall know Me, from the least of them to the greatest of them. 12 For I will be merciful to their unrighteousness, and their sins and their lawless deeds I will remember no more." 13 In that He says, "A new covenant," He has made the first obsolete. Now what is becoming obsolete and growing old is ready to vanish away.

Okay, the new covenant was not designed as behavior modification. The new covenant was to be a much deeper work. God was not going to merely give sinful people rules to follow. He was going to write His ways on their very hearts!

Also notice the aspect of this new covenant involving the lawless deeds otherwise known as sins. God says He will be merciful and choose to forget their sins, referring to those who would enter the new covenant.

This is amazing! God opened a way for unrighteous people to enter into a new covenant with Him. The first covenant was God's way of proving to humanity that they were dead without Him. The new covenant is God providing a way for dead humanity to become alive! The blood of Jesus paid for this amazing new covenant!

So we've been using this word covenant a lot. Did you know that you could also use the word "testament?" Check out one of the definitions from Dictionary.com for the word testament:

"A covenant instituted between God and man, esp. the covenant of Moses or that instituted by Christ."

Isn't that interesting? This may give some insight into the Bible. Notice that it's broken into two major sections. The first part is known as what? The Old Testament! The second part is known as the New Testament.

Please look at Hebrews 9 to gain some spiritual enlightenment on this.

Hebrews 9:16-17
For where there is a testament, there must also of necessity be the death of the testator.

17 For a testament is in force after men are dead, since it has no power at all while the testator lives.

Okay, so this sounds kind of strange. You understand what a "last will and testament" is, right? Someone who has personal property or belongings creates a legal agreement that decrees who gains possession of their stuff when they die. That legal document is called the last will and testament.

For the sake of illustration, let's say you are old and you have one son and one daughter. Now let's say that you have a will that states your son will get your horses and your daughter will get your house. Let me ask you this. When do your kids get your stuff? (The answer is after you die.)

The Bible is simply making this point. God made a will and testament and it went into effect when Jesus died. The blood of Jesus sealed the new covenant!

It's very important that you and I receive Jesus. We have no covenant with God apart from what Jesus paid for on the cross. Your good works cannot save you. You and I need Jesus.

I remember preaching about the heart of God to some young people (mostly between the ages of eleven and seventeen) in Lagos, Nigeria. The message was called "The Father's Heart," and I delivered it on Father's Day in 2014. I had not planned that message to coincide with Father's Day, it just worked out that way.

Actually, I knew that the message God had given me was for those students. It's a good message for anybody, but I feel especially inclined to deliver it to people in Nigeria when the opportunity arises.

When I preached it to those thirteen students, two of them raised their hands to receive Jesus! It was awesome! There is nothing like watching people get saved. It is a great privilege that God has allowed me to witness many, many times. God has made me a soul-winner! This is something I didn't deserve, but the blood of Jesus brought God's grace and favor into my life!

Let's continue reading in Hebrews chapter 9.

Hebrews 9:18-22
Therefore not even the first covenant was dedicated without blood. 19 For when Moses had spoken every precept to all the people according to the law, he took the blood of calves and goats, with water, scarlet wool, and hyssop, and sprinkled both the book itself and all the people, 20 saying, "This is the blood of the covenant which God has commanded

you." 21 Then likewise he sprinkled with blood both the tabernacle and all the vessels of the ministry. 22 And according to the law almost all things are purified with blood, and without shedding of blood there is no remission.

God established the first covenant with blood. God is smart. He knew that it was going to take the sacrifice of His own Son to complete the everlasting covenant. With the first covenant, God proved to us that we cannot fulfill His will in our own strength. He also used blood to give us a picture of what the ultimate solution would look like.

The ultimate solution for our sinful natures would come through the sacrifice of blood. It would not however, be the blood of animals, it would be the blood of God's Son! The blood of Jesus is the solution for the fallen state of mankind!

Here are two very interesting verses to compare side by side:

Acts 20:28
Therefore take heed to yourselves and to all the flock, among which the Holy Spirit has made you overseers, to shepherd the church of God which He purchased with His own blood.

Hebrews 2:14
Inasmuch then as the children have partaken of flesh and blood, He Himself likewise shared in the same, that through death He might destroy him who had the power of death, that is, the devil,

In **Acts 20:28** we read that God purchased the church with **"His own blood."** In **Hebrews 2:14** it declares that Jesus shared the same flesh and blood of humanity as we have. I would look at one verse and say Jesus has the blood of God. After reading the other verse I would say He has the blood of humanity. Could both be true?

Jesus referred to Himself as the Son of Man. We also know Him as the Son of God. Jesus came in the flesh. This is how Jesus is known as the Son of Man. Jesus is also known as the Son of God. Since God is His Father, Jesus had the characteristics of His Father. Jesus was spiritually alive!

These things are great mysteries! We can know for sure that the Son of God gave His blood to save sinful humanity!

Hebrews 10:5-7
Therefore, when He came into the world, He said: "Sacrifice and offering You did not desire, But a body You have prepared for Me. 6 In burnt offerings and sacrifices for sin You

had no pleasure. 7 Then I said, 'Behold, I have come— In the volume of the book it is written of Me— To do Your will, O God.'"

These were prophetic words. Jesus was the one who came to do the will of God. He came to finish His Father's will concerning the new covenant.

Hebrews 10:8-10
Previously saying, "Sacrifice and offering, burnt offerings, and offerings for sin You did not desire, nor had pleasure in them" (which are offered according to the law), 9 then He said, "Behold, I have come to do Your will, O God." He takes away the first that He may establish the second. 10 By that will we have been sanctified through the offering of the body of Jesus Christ once for all.

Jesus established the second covenant. Understand that this is the final covenant. There will be no third covenant. When Jesus said it is finished, His blood sealed the new covenant which was established on better promises!

The new covenant is everlasting. It is sealed! The first covenant had a fault. Sinful people could not keep their end of the deal. So God sent His Son. Jesus came to the earth and fulfilled His Father's will. He was our mediator! He was the one who performed God's will perfectly. As He gave His life, the covenant was sealed as perfect and complete. There is no fault in the new covenant. Jesus sealed it with His faultless blood!

Now through this everlasting agreement that Jesus sealed with God and humanity through his blood, we have good works to do! Notice the proper order of this. The good works we do are not the basis of the covenant. This has already been sealed by the blood of God's Son. Our good works come after we enter into this covenant. We enter into the everlasting covenant through faith in Jesus.

Ephesians 2:8-10
For by grace you have been saved through faith, and that not of yourselves; it is the gift of God, 9 not of works, lest anyone should boast. 10 For we are His workmanship, created in Christ Jesus for good works, which God prepared beforehand that we should walk in them.

Those of us who have placed our faith in God's Son now have things to do in our lifetimes! We get to shine His light and watch people glorify our Father in Heaven. We get to walk in partnership with Him to establish His will upon the earth!

1 Corinthians 3:9
For we are God's fellow workers; you are

God's field, you are God's building.

Understand as you are in this amazing grace, that there are great things in store for you. God is the leader and He calls us fellow workers! It will blow your mind if you let it! It is an amazing privilege to partner with God and help Him establish His will on the earth.

Matthew 6:9-10
In this manner, therefore, pray: Our Father in heaven, Hallowed be Your name. 10 Your kingdom come. Your will be done, On earth as it is in heaven.

Jesus wanted us to pray that the will of God would be done on the earth as it is in Heaven. How is the will of God done in Heaven? I would say it is done perfectly. This is the way we should pray. This is also the way we should live.

I remember going on an evangelistic outreach in Lagos, Nigeria. I talked with about five or so people by a particular store. One Muslim man gave his life to Jesus that day! A single mother of two little boys also prayed to be saved. Another guy, who was a taxi driver, was already saved, but he asked me to pray that his taxi business would increase. I prayed for him, but I thought to myself that if I ever needed a ride I would give him a call.

It turned out that at some point, my normal mode of transportation wasn't available, so I gave that taxi driver a call and paid him for a ride. Since then, I've paid for more rides and have had some very insightful conversations with him about Nigerian politics and infrastructural concerns.

My point is this; Jesus didn't just want us to pray high and lofty prayers that sound good but mean nothing. He wanted us to pray that the will of God would be brought down to earth. Understand that we are the hands and feet of Jesus. He operates on this earth through us. He needs our willing hearts to carry out his plans here. He wants to work through you and me to accomplish great things!

John 14:12-13
"Most assuredly, I say to you, he who believes in Me, the works that I do he will do also; and greater works than these he will do, because I go to My Father. 13 And whatever you ask in My name, that I will do, that the Father may be glorified in the Son.

God has great works for each of us to do. The everlasting covenant has been sealed with the blood of Jesus. Through faith in Jesus we get to operate with authority on the earth! Together in partnership with God, we get to perform the great works of His divine pleasure!

Hebrews 13:20-21

Now may the God of peace who brought up our Lord Jesus from the dead, that great Shepherd of the sheep, through the blood of the everlasting covenant, 21 make you complete in every good work to do His will, working in you what is well pleasing in His sight, through Jesus Christ, to whom be glory forever and ever. Amen.

The blood of Jesus sealed the everlasting covenant. Are you in the everlasting covenant?

Chapter Five
His Blood Gives Access

Hebrews 4:14-16
Seeing then that we have a great High Priest who has passed through the heavens, Jesus the Son of God, let us hold fast our confession. 15 For we do not have a High Priest who cannot sympathize with our weaknesses, but was in all points tempted as we are, yet without sin. 16 Let us therefore come boldly to the throne of grace, that we may obtain mercy and find grace to help in time of need.

We have direct access to God because of the blood of Jesus! We can come boldly to the throne of what? It's not wrath. We don't need to squeamishly cower before the throne of justice. No! Through the amazing love of God we can come boldly, with confidence, to the throne of grace.

As a quick tangent, can I ask you if you are

43

allowing grace to have a majestic place in your life? Do you walk in the reality of God's grace? Are you showing grace to others?

One of the saddest things I've seen in the church world is legalism. Usually people identify this as religion. That is usually how it plays out, but there is a good type of religion.

James 1:27
Pure and undefiled religion before God and the Father is this: to visit orphans and widows in their trouble, and to keep oneself unspotted from the world.

This makes me want to go on another tangent, so here goes. I figure if you have read this book up until this point, you're probably going to finish it, so why not take a bunny trail or two?

We as Christians are called to take care of widows and orphans in their trouble. When are they in trouble? Right after they have lost their loved ones. That initial time can be extremely urgent. They may need help for a long time afterward.

Our Father's view of pure religion has to do with us resisting evil and visiting orphans and widows in their trouble. We don't need to hide from them. We don't need to have a depraved indifference to their pain or their needs. Do you want to do some of the good works that Jesus talked about? If so, find a way to visit orphans and widows through your time and finances. You'll be amazed at how God will pay you back!

Okay, let me go back to my first bunny trail. I was going to make this point; legalism sucks! Let me tell you why I don't like legalism by first defining it clearly.

Legalism (as defined by Sam Hager) is the process of forcefully imposing ceremonial works upon someone in order to control and manipulate them, under the guise of earning privileges with God. Legalistic religious leaders want power over people and do not want them to freely receive God's grace.

Here are the two main reasons I HATE legalistic religion:

1. **Because it's demonic.**
2. **Because it interferes with the relationship between humans and their Creator.**

Okay, let me go back to the original topic of this chapter. It's about accessing rights and privileges available to us through the blood of Jesus. Notice that **Hebrews 4:14** said, **"Seeing then that we**

have a great High Priest who has passed
through the heavens, Jesus the Son of God, let
us hold fast our confession."

When Jesus passed through the heavens, He
went with His blood to the holiest place of all! He
did this once for all. He is the mediator between
God and mankind! He paid for us to have access
to God.

Hebrews 9:24-28

For Christ has not entered the holy places
made with hands, which are copies of the true,
but into heaven itself, now to appear in the
presence of God for us; 25 not that He should
offer Himself often, as the high priest enters
the Most Holy Place every year with blood of
another— 26 He then would have had to
suffer often since the foundation of the world;
but now, once at the end of the ages, He has
appeared to put away sin by the sacrifice of
Himself. 27 And as it is appointed for men to
die once, but after this the judgment, 28 so
Christ was offered once to bear the sins of
many. To those who eagerly wait for Him He
will appear a second time, apart from sin, for
salvation.

Understand that the blood of Jesus speaks good
things for you. It gives life and has the power to
wash away your sins. The blood of Jesus also

sealed the everlasting covenant with God. All of this is available to you, but you have to receive it. God doesn't force this upon anybody. We can choose to receive what Jesus paid for with His blood.

Likewise, we have an inheritance and access to divine promises through the blood of Jesus. These rights and privileges are available, but are not forced upon us. We need to approach the throne of grace boldly and receive all that God has for us. It is very possible that many privileges and miracles go unclaimed and therefore not received because we don't obtain them. They are available, but we don't take advantage of the rights we have as sons and daughters of the Most High God.

Let us be the children of God who access all of what God has paid for. Let us not allow any blessing to sit around when we could rightfully benefit from it. Jesus paid a huge price to give us access to the throne of grace. Let us come boldly. This is His will for us.

Ephesians 1:3
Blessed be the God and Father of our Lord Jesus Christ, who has blessed us with every spiritual blessing in the heavenly places in Christ,

God is blessed and He has blessed us! You have

heard that you are "blessed to be a blessing," right? That comes through the divine nature. He is blessed and He has privileged us with every spiritual provision! These blessings are in the heavenly places, and are available to those of us who are in Christ.

When Jesus shed His blood on the cross, He paid for you and me to have access to every spiritual blessing! The work has been done by Jesus and the covenant is sealed. God doesn't want us to try to work for access so that we may be granted a privilege or two. No! Jesus has done the complete work. Every, every, every spiritual blessing is freely available to you through the blood of Jesus!

Keep in mind also that God doesn't want us to seek blessings, spiritual enlightenment, spiritual gifts, or powers through any other way. Jesus is the way! He is the only way! Everything you need is found in Christ and in Him alone!

I have a brutally painful story that highlights the dangers of seeking means other than through Jesus to gain special insight and abilities. I used to be good friends with someone. We worked together in ministry and really enjoyed hanging out. He was funny and full of practical wisdom. I gained a lot through my relationship with him.

At some point though, he started veering away from the truth of God's Word. He felt that he lacked in certain areas, so he started reading books full of occultism and witchcraft. I don't know how it all escalated but before I knew it, he was telling me he had discovered things that enlightened him beyond the mentality that he previously knew.

I distinctly remember one of our conversations in which he cussed in reference to certain ministers that he had once learned from. The demonic books which he had allowed to corrupt his mind had introduced bitterness toward people of influence. He actually believed that prominent preachers were keeping secrets away from the general public as to how they became successful.

It was heartbreaking to me that as I tried to reason with him gently and through love, he dug his heels in to the new "knowledge" that he had discovered. He became committed to turning his back on what he knew was right so he could fully embrace demonic lies. It was truly not easy for me to walk sadly away from my relationship with him. He was a great friend at one point, but if he wants that kind of a life then I have to love him from a distance. I want the best for him, but he's his own person and has his own decisions to make. My prayer is that he turns back to the simplicity of God and God's love for him. Could you pray for my former friend? God knows who

I'm talking about.

Hebrews 12:14-15
Pursue peace with all people, and holiness,
without which no one will see the Lord: 15
looking carefully lest anyone fall short of the
grace of God; lest any root of bitterness
springing up cause trouble, and by this many
become defiled;

Don't fall short of grace. Fall into grace. In fact
I'd say fall into the grace of God with reckless
abandon. One big thing that will defile us is
bitterness. A series of commercials aired years ago
about not having bitter beer face. Well, I don't
know about you, but I think I've seen my share of
bitter Christian faces. This should not be so!
Forgiveness is vital for your spiritual well-being.
Don't block yourself from the promises of God
through resentment!

You and I will be hurt by others. It's a fact. We
will have opportunities to become upset with
somebody and not let go of the offense. People
will do dumb things, just as we ourselves will be
prone to do. If we're not careful we will reduce our
faith and limit what we receive from God through
bitterness. We need to let the same type of words
that the blood of Jesus speaks on our behalf come
from our mouths toward those who hurt us. It
may seem impossible to forgive that person who

hurt you, but with God, all things are possible. You can walk in love and forgiveness through the power of the blood of Jesus.

If you are identifying someone now that you are holding a grudge against, then talk with God and ask Him to help you let them go. Determine that your destiny is not worth handing over to the enemy because of hurts and offenses. Don't allow your love to grow cold because of the mistakes of others. Be victorious in this life through the blood of Jesus!

So if we are going to access what is rightfully ours through the blood of Jesus, we need to know what His promises are. Once again, this is where getting into God's Word is crucial.

1 Peter 2:2
as newborn babes, desire the pure milk of the word, that you may grow thereby,

This should be the way we desire the Word of God. We need to crave it all of our lives! So many times this verse has been used while talking about new believers. But it's not saying this exclusively to new believers in Christ. Notice it starts off by saying, "**as.**" This is comparing something that we understand naturally to something spiritual. Whether we are new to the faith or have been rockin' with Jesus for a while, we need to desire the pure milk of the Word so that we can grow!

When we get into God's Word, we uncover promises and realities that we did not previously know. God has treasure inside of His Word. He wants you and me to discover it. He's not going to keep it hidden if you want to search for it. The question is, "Do you want to seek after it until you find it?"

Matthew 7:7-8
"Ask, and it will be given to you; seek, and you will find; knock, and it will be opened to you. 8 For everyone who asks receives, and he who seeks finds, and to him who knocks it will be opened."

Ask God to reveal what belongs to you as a believer in Christ. Seek for the treasures that are found in Him. Knock on the door of Heaven, so to speak (reminds me of a song). Search out the scriptures, ask God for insight and keep pressing in!

Ephesians 1:7
In Him we have redemption through His blood, the forgiveness of sins, according to the riches of His grace

There are rights and privileges you have access to through the blood of Jesus. Find out what they

are through His Word. Ask God to enlighten your
spiritual eyes so you can see what belongs to you!

Chapter Six
His Blood Sets Us Apart

Hebrews 10:19-22

Therefore, brethren, having boldness to enter the Holiest by the blood of Jesus, 20 by a new and living way which He consecrated for us, through the veil, that is, His flesh, 21 and having a High Priest over the house of God, 22 let us draw near with a true heart in full assurance of faith, having our hearts sprinkled from an evil conscience and our bodies washed with pure water.

We can have boldness to enter the throne room of grace and we can have boldness to enter the Holiest by the blood of Jesus! This is beyond amazing! If you remember the things written in the Old Testament, then this should make you tremendously thankful to God. Back then, there was only one appointed high priest who could enter the holiest place of the tabernacle once per year.

There's an element of doubt that can try to disguise itself as respect when it comes to this. Be careful that you don't fall into the trap of keeping yourself back from the throne of grace because you think it's too good for you. The blood of Jesus has opened wide the door to the throne room for you! His blood has given life and provided a way for you to be clean. The everlasting covenant has been established and will not be revoked! Because of the blood of Jesus, you can enter the most holy place!

Let me take this a step further. God wants you to enter His throne room. He doesn't want you to hold yourself back. He has amazing things for you and it gives Him pleasure when you enter this place. It is a majestic place where worry and lack do not exist. Jesus is your sufficiency and fear is nowhere to be found. God wants you close to Him!

I believe in visions and dreams. They are all through the Bible. Some people today say that these things are not for our modern era. I try not to entangle myself in such ridiculous arguments. I let the foolishness of God confound the wise in the world. I'll gladly look foolish to doubters and haters as I seek after spiritual gifts and blessings. I don't seek after them just to soak them in greedily. The truth is that it gets easy to bless others when I myself am blessed. Spiritual gifts are designed to bring glory to God and help people. I don't want to fight against anything that God wants to give me. If He has more for me, then I want it! That is not greed, that is faith. He is good and He gives good gifts!

I've asked God for visions. They didn't come immediately and I haven't experienced hundreds of them, but God has given me some. One time as I prayed, a vision of a hexagonal pattern became apparent to me. I saw what looked like a grey honeycomb. Instead of the shapes having shallow concaves like the honeycombs bees make, these were like pipes that extended beyond where I could see.

I asked God for insight into the vision and received simply this. The hexagonal pattern represented the body of Christ. We are all connected and there is no schism in the body. The fact that every shape was like a pipe or tunnel was symbolic of how the blessings of Heaven flow through us into the world.

If that story didn't make you think I'm crazy, then let me tell you about another vision that God gave me. I was at a minister's conference in Arkansas in my early 20's. At that conference, we had hours of praise and worship. It was great! I love to praise my God! In our extended worship,

God let me see the white horse that Jesus would return on. The horse was majestic and muscular, but as I observed the beautiful white horse, Jesus opened His eyes of fire in front of me! There is no way to describe how powerful His eyes are! I collapsed. I laid on the carpet, and after a while He let me see in the natural again. I was looking under the pews of the church and I was like, "Whoa!"

Gently I felt God ask me if I would like to look into his eyes again. In that holy moment I said, "Yes." He opened His eyes to me once again. This time instead of an inferno in His eyes, it was as if they were giant windows. He allowed me to come close to the window and look through His eyes! I saw what He saw. In the vision, a huge crowd of people was gathered together. It was dark around them. The sea of believers had their hands raised. Jesus was looking at His people and they were worshiping Him! That was the extent of the vision.

Looking into the eyes of Jesus was the most intense thing I have ever experienced. There is no way to fully describe the power and majesty of our Lord and King! Afterward, I could barely move. I wasn't scared, but in a deep place of awe and wonder! In that place of wonder I gained the insight that we must love what He loves and hate what He hates.

Hebrews 10:23-25

Let us hold fast the confession of our hope without wavering, for He who promised is faithful. 24 And let us consider one another in order to stir up love and good works, 25 not forsaking the assembling of ourselves together, as is the manner of some, but exhorting one another, and so much the more as you see the Day approaching.

Let us not be silent! God has amazing promises and He is faithful. In this blood-soaked Christian life, we should be mindful of other believers and encourage them to do good things. Stir up love and good works!

I remember years ago when I lived with my parents in the country, we would burn our trash in metal burn barrels. Admittedly, it was fun to watch the garbage go up in smoke! After some time the blaze died down and piles of ashes remained. We would take sticks and stir the ashes around, then the fire would erupt again. This is similar to what I picture when the Bible talks about stirring up love and good works.

We are not trash, burning in barrels. We are on fire with God's presence! Sometimes life can be hard and relentlessly monotonous. We need to stir each other up! A great way for this to happen is by assembling together. Meeting with other believers is a part of God's spiritual growth plan for you and me.

I have seen a lot of people shipwreck their lives by walking away from church. We should not be stuck in dead religion, but we need to assemble with others who exhibit and promote the life of Jesus! Be careful not to remove yourself from church just because it's not exactly perfect. The church is comprised of people like you and me. We are all prone to mistakes. Understand that we are set apart, not because we are perfect, but because we have received Jesus and He has received us.

Hebrews 13:10-12
We have an altar from which those who serve the tabernacle have no right to eat. 11 For the bodies of those animals, whose blood is brought into the sanctuary by the high priest for sin, are burned outside the camp. 12 Therefore Jesus also, that He might sanctify the people with His own blood, suffered outside the gate.

The word "sanctify" means to set apart for a holy purpose. You and I have been set apart so we can be partners with God in establishing His will on the earth. We are His children who tell the world about our loving heavenly Father.

Some will not believe us. They think what we offer is foolishness. Realize that we are set apart. This means we are not just set apart to something, but also from something. We are not the same as the world. We are different and those who refuse to believe in Jesus will persecute and try to stop what they don't agree with.

I have had the opportunity to lead many people to Jesus! I've seen people respond to the goodness of God in churches, in parks, in cars, at sporting events, while walking on the street, in homes, and one day soon I believe I'll see it on an airplane! God is good!

Sometimes I run across people who hate my guts. They can't stand what I'm talking about. People have yelled at me and told me to go away. I don't argue with people. Arguing is a man-made mental battle of words. I'm not interested in arguing, so I politely leave if someone doesn't want me around.

One time in particular illustrates this very well. I was driving with my wife and son and I noticed an elderly lady sitting on the sidewalk. She appeared to be talking with herself and she looked rough. I felt for her so I turned the car around and parked close to where she was. I sat down by her and she asked, "Why do you want to sit next to an ugly old woman like me?" I said, "No, you're not ugly." I talked to her while my wife and son waited in the car with the windows rolled down not very far away. The woman and I chatted for a while and then I said something like, "You know the Bible says..."

She immediately cut me off. "That's why you're here!" She yelled at me. She started saying all sorts of weird things like I probably have the Bible tattooed on my legs. She was really upset!

My kid freaked out. He was pretty young at the time, and he had never experienced someone snapping like that. He started to cry and rolled up his window. My wife said that she thought we should leave, so we did just that. We did pray for her as we left, though. I hope she turns to the truth before it's too late.

It's very natural to be persecuted for doing what is right. Jesus said to rejoice and be glad when this happens. God doesn't want you to be discouraged. Just because one person does not receive your message of hope, that doesn't mean that the next person won't gladly hear what you have to say. Stay encouraged! God is with His people! You are not alone!

Hebrews 10:13-16
Therefore let us go forth to Him, outside the

camp, bearing His reproach. 14 For here we have no continuing city, but we seek the one to come. 15 Therefore by Him let us continually offer the sacrifice of praise to God, that is, the fruit of our lips, giving thanks to His name. 16 But do not forget to do good and to share, for with such sacrifices God is well pleased.

Heaven is our home! Let us not get too attached to this temporary place. Heaven is our home and Heaven is real! Praise Jesus! We don't have to go to Hell! Even though Hell is what we deserve for our sinfulness, the blood of Jesus speaks good things for us!

We have a lot to be thankful for. We should praise God continually for the blood of Jesus! We should thank Jesus for going to the cross for us! He is awesome! Thank You Jesus!

God also wants us to do good works and share His gospel with people here on the earth. He has a purpose for you and me. Let us be all about our Father's business! There are sick people to lay hands on so God can heal them! There are lost people who need to hear us tell them the good news so they can be saved! There are people in prison who need to know that Jesus offers forgiveness and spiritual freedom! There are those without basic necessities who need us as believers in Christ to help them.

The blood of Jesus is what you and I need! His blood speaks for us. His blood gives us life and washes our sins away! The blood of Jesus sealed the everlasting covenant. Through His blood we have access to the throne of grace. We can enter the holiest place through the blood of Jesus!

The choice is ours to make individually. What do you choose?

Chapter Seven

His Blood Is Our Confession

We are now at the climax of this entire book! The teaching contained in the previous pages is not intended to remain inactive. The blood of Jesus has the power to transform your very existence!

This last chapter is all about identifying with the One who gave His blood so that we could become children of God. The following is a list of confessions that you and I can make concerning the blood of Jesus. Let me encourage you to take your time and say each of these statements out loud!

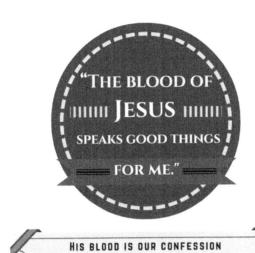

"THE BLOOD OF JESUS SPEAKS GOOD THINGS FOR ME."

HIS BLOOD IS OUR CONFESSION

His Blood Is Our Confession

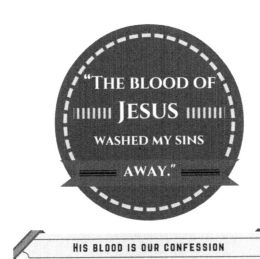

"THE BLOOD OF JESUS WASHED MY SINS AWAY."

HIS BLOOD IS OUR CONFESSION

His Blood Is Our Confession

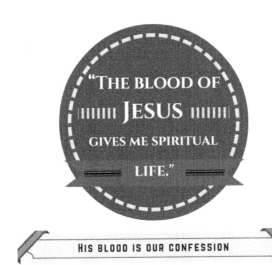

"THE BLOOD OF JESUS GIVES ME SPIRITUAL LIFE."

HIS BLOOD IS OUR CONFESSION

His Blood Is Our Confession

"I AM IN COVENANT with God through the blood of His Son."

HIS BLOOD IS OUR CONFESSION

His Blood Is Our Confession

"I AM
SET APART
BY
THE BLOOD
OF JESUS."

HIS BLOOD IS OUR CONFESSION

His Blood Is Our Confession

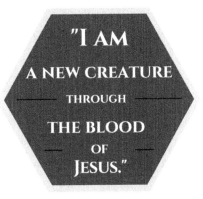

"I AM
A NEW CREATURE
— THROUGH —
THE BLOOD
— OF —
JESUS."

HIS BLOOD IS OUR CONFESSION

"I AM
AN AMBASSADOR
—— OF GOD ——
THROUGH THE BLOOD
—— OF ——
JESUS."

HIS BLOOD IS OUR CONFESSION

His Blood Is Our Confession

"SPIRITUAL AUTHORITY
IS MINE THROUGH
THE BLOOD OF JESUS."

HIS BLOOD IS OUR CONFESSION

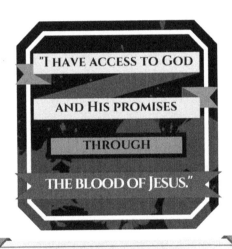

"I HAVE ACCESS TO GOD AND HIS PROMISES THROUGH THE BLOOD OF JESUS."

HIS BLOOD IS OUR CONFESSION

"I WALK FORGIVEN
AND IN NEWNESS OF LIFE
THROUGH
THE BLOOD OF JESUS."

HIS BLOOD IS OUR CONFESSION

"THANK YOU

FATHER

FOR THE BLOOD

OF YOUR SON

JESUS!"

HIS BLOOD IS OUR CONFESSION

His Blood Is Our Confession

"THANK YOU

JESUS

FOR SHEDDING

YOUR BLOOD

FOR ME!"

HIS BLOOD IS OUR CONFESSION

His Blood Is Our Confession

Closing

I have great news to share with those who have not yet called on Jesus. He is the Son of God! We are lost without Him, but He doesn't want us to be lost. Jesus gave His life for our sins. He paid the price so we could be forgiven and brought into the family of God!

As Christians, we are not our own. We have been purchased. This was a voluntary arrangement, designed by God. Jesus willingly gave His life to save us. We used our freedom of will to choose Jesus and declare Him as the Lord of our lives. Now that the price has been paid and we have allowed Jesus to pay for us, we are not our own. In other words, we belong to Jesus and He is our loving leader!

1 Corinthians 6:19-20
Or do you not know that your body is the temple of the Holy Spirit who is in you, whom you have from God, and you are not your own? 20 For you were bought at a price;

therefore glorify God in your body and in your spirit, which are God's.

God wants to bring transformation throughout the entirety of your life. As Christians we represent Jesus to a world of people who are lost. Remember, God loves them as He loves you. The same grace that you did not earn is available to everyone else.

Jesus said that He did not come to condemn the world, but to save the world. As followers of Jesus, we are to help Jesus gather people for the Kingdom of Heaven. If Jesus did not condemn the lost, neither should we. Our job is to tell others about the free grace of God.

Also, there is good news for us to enjoy. God loves us! He has never stopped! As Christians, we need to understand what has happened for us. On our behalf the blood of Jesus:

- **Speaks for us**
- **Washes us**
- **Gives us life**
- **Sealed the new covenant**
- **Gives us free access to God**
- **Sets us apart**

This is good news for Christians! Who is like

our God? He is amazing and He loves us deeply! Thank You Jesus for giving Your blood! You are amazing!

Prayer

God loves you! If you have never received the free gift of salvation, now is the perfect time. The Bible makes it clear that we are completely hopeless without God. We have all sinned and need a savior. God sent His Son Jesus to be that Savior.

In **John 14:6** Jesus said, **"I am the way, the truth, and the life. No one comes to the Father except through Me."**

Jesus died on the cross to pay the price for our sinfulness. God raised Him from the dead 3 days later! Jesus brought His blood before the Father as the perfect sacrifice for us. His blood speaks good things for us!

Romans 10:9-11
that if you confess with your mouth the Lord Jesus and believe in your heart that God has raised Him from the dead, you will be saved. 10 For with the heart one believes unto

righteousness, and with the mouth confession is made unto salvation. 11 For the Scripture says, "Whoever believes on Him will not be put to shame."

Are you ready to call on Jesus? He will save you and make you brand new.

If you want to receive Jesus now, simply believe that God raised Jesus from the dead and say, "Jesus is Lord!"

Made in the USA
Middletown, DE
16 November 2022

15042634R00060